Contents

Words in **bold** are in the glossary on page 28.

All about me

My name is Madina Ibrahimi and I am ten years old. I was born in Kabul, the capital of Afghanistan. My family became **refugees** and now I live in Fulham, West London. At home we speak **Dari**, our Afghan language.

I'm a keen cook. Every weekend I cook Afghan food and other dishes.

Moving to Britain from
Afghanistan

By Cath Senker
Photography by Howard Davies

FRANKLIN WATTS

First published in 2008 by Franklin Watts

Franklin Watts,
338 Euston Road,
London, NW1 3BH

Franklin Watts Australia,
Level 17/207 Kent Street,
Sydney, NSW 2000

Series editor: Sarah Peutrill
Art director: Jonathan Hair
Design: Rita Storey
Photographs: Howard Davies (unless otherwise stated)

Acknowledgements:
The author and photographer would like to thank the following for
their help in the preparation of this book: The Afghan Association,
London; Huggy, Rebecca and the students at Greenhouse
Schools Project, St Paul's Girls' School; Dlawar, Ghazal, Gullsanga,
Madina and Mina Ibrahimi; Vanessa Dymitrow, Sue Hayward,
Catherine Jaramillo, Adam Young, and all the staff and students
at Sir John Lillie Primary School, London; Zia Salemi.

Picture credits: We would like to thank the Ibrahimi family for
permission to reproduce photographs on the following pages:
cover (inset), 12, 15 and 25b. Bruno Pagnanelli/Shutterstock: 10b
Marcel Mettelsiefen/Shutterstock: 11.

Dewey number: 304.8'41'0581

ISBN: 978 0 7496 7858 6

Printed in China

Franklin Watts is a division of Hachette Children's Books, an
Hachette Livre UK company.
www.hachettelivre.co.uk

My friend Vanessa and I make up our own dance routines.

I enjoy lots of other activities. I love all kinds of dancing, including Afghan and belly dancing. Often I make up songs and dance routines with my friends. I also like junk modelling.

Try speaking in Dari!

Hello
Salaam

Goodbye
Khodo hafez

How are you?
Chutor asti?

I'm fine, thank you
Khub astem, tashakur

(Look out for more Dari words in this book.)

I'm making a necklace. Recently, I made a jewellery box and some wire toys.

Meet my family

Here is my family. Ghazal is on my right. My sisters and I are wearing our traditional Afghan dresses.

I live with my dad, Dlawar, and my mum, Gullsanga. Dad isn't working at the moment. He helps us all at home, and he is a fantastic cook. Mum is studying **beauty therapy** at college and works part time in an office.

I have two sisters. Ghazal is 16 and Mina is 14.

Mum's brother, Uncle Zia, lives in London but most of her family are in California, USA. Most of Dad's relatives are in Afghanistan.

Family words

Mother	*Madar*
Father	*Padar*
Brother	*Brodar*
Sister	*Khohar*
Grandmother	*Beebee*
Grandfather	*Bobo*

We usually eat Afghan food at home. My uncle Zia has come to visit us.

About Afghanistan

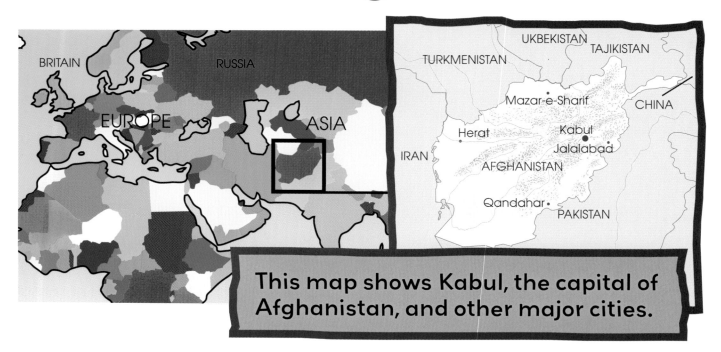

This map shows Kabul, the capital of Afghanistan, and other major cities.

Afghanistan is in Asia. It lies between Pakistan and Iran. In 1979, Afghanistan was **invaded** by the **Soviet Union**. There was a long **civil war**. Many people were killed and millions forced to leave their homes. The war continued after the Soviet forces left in 1989.

Kabul lies in a valley between two steep mountain ranges.

In 1996 the **Taliban** seized Kabul. The Taliban brought in an extreme form of **Islamic** rule. Women were not allowed to go out to work, and girls could not go to school.

In 2001, a US-led force defeated the Taliban. Since then fighting between the new government and the Taliban has continued.

Madina's sister Ghazal says:

"In Afghanistan, firstly the fighting has to stop. Women should have the same rights as men, and there should be education for all."

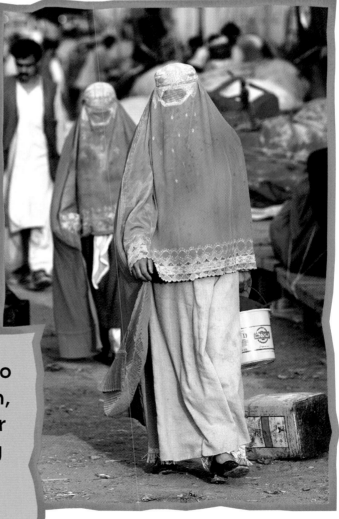

Although the Taliban no longer rule Afghanistan, many women still cover themselves with a long cloak called a **burka** when they go out.

My life in Afghanistan

We lived through many terrifying years of war in Kabul. After the Taliban victory, we girls and Mum had to stay at home, but we were better off than many. Dad ran a restaurant and a transport hire company. We had enough money and a big house, where we lived with our **extended family**.

Ghazal and Mina in our home in Kabul, wearing Afghan dresses.

This is us when we lived in Kabul – with me asleep!

However, my family was in danger from the Taliban. They arrested my grandad and we knew Dad would be next. We had to escape.

Madina's mum Gullsanga says:

"During the war I was always worried. I took the girls with me from room to room in the house because I was so scared of the rocket attacks. At night we all slept together to feel safe."

Mum has many photos of our life back in Afghanistan. I can't remember much, so mum and my sisters tell me all about it.

Moving to Britain

This is a view of the estate in Fulham where we live now.

It was a really long journey to Britain. I can't remember much because I was only three at the time.

First we went to Tajikistan, north of Afghanistan. From there we took the train to Russia. When we arrived in Russia, it was snowing.

Counting in Dari

1 *Yak*
2 *Duh*
3 *Ce*
4 *Chor*
5 *Panj*
6 *Shash*
7 *Haft*
8 *Asht*
9 *Nuh*
10 *Dah*

We continued our journey overland across Europe, travelling with other Afghans. We went on many trains and buses.

Finally, we crossed from France to Britain on a boat. It was an exhausting journey.

This is me (right) with my sister Mina in a coffee shop the day after we arrived in Britain.

My new hometown

We enjoy walking in Ravenscourt Park, near where we used to live in Shepherd's Bush.

When we arrived in Britain, we claimed **asylum** as refugees. We were sent to West London, first to Shepherd's Bush and then here to Fulham.

Madina's mum says:

"At first, none of us could speak English. People were kind, and we felt positive. The **housing officer** said to me, 'You've got a smiling face, so everyone will help you!'"

I'm getting into reading now and go to the library every week.

It felt safer in Britain. We could go to school, the park and the leisure centre and we felt free. My sisters and I made friends with all kinds of people. In Afghanistan we couldn't even go to the shops.

We live quite close to a large exhibition centre.

There are some dangers here though. There are some problems on the estate. Mum won't let us go out alone.

Going to school

Here I am with some of my friends. I get on well with everyone in my class.

I started school in Reception. My sisters started in Year 5 and Year 3. They had never been to school before so it was very hard for them at first. All of us fitted in quickly at school and made friends.

At break and lunchtime we play tag. Sometimes we make up songs and dances.

When I started school, I had extra help to learn English. My teacher, Miss Compton, taught me all the basic words and kept repeating them until I remembered what they meant. By Year 2, I had caught up with my class.

Madina's sister Mina says:

"At first, I couldn't understand a word the teacher said. When she asked me something, I just said 'Uh?' After school each day, she read with me for five minutes, which gave me the boost I needed. Now I'm doing better than many English kids in my class!"

Mum takes me to school in the morning, and Ghazal or Mina usually picks me up.

My school day

In PE we sometimes play dodge ball. If you hit someone in the other team with the big ball, that person is out.

When we moved to Fulham, I started at Sir John Lillie Primary School. There are other Afghans as well as kids from the Caribbean, India, Pakistan, Egypt and Poland.

Maths is my best subject – I love numbers and working out problems. PE is my other favourite lesson. I also like science and history.

Madina's teacher, Mr Young, says:
"Madina is positive and enthusiastic and she's strongly involved in all aspects of school life."

I'm not so fond of literacy because I find it difficult.

On Friday mornings, we can choose our activities. We can draw cartoons, make cakes, do arts and crafts, or street dancing.

My teacher is Mr Young. He is helping me to improve in literacy.

I enjoy the healthy school dinners at our school.

21

Free time

I spend much of my free time doing sport. I go to after-school clubs to do basketball, football and **martial arts**. On Saturday I go to a sports club with my sisters to do basketball training. I'm the youngest there, but I keep up!

Madina's sister Ghazal says:

"It's been easy to fit in here. At school and in our local area there are people from countries all over the world. It's very **multicultural**."

Basketball training is tough – but I love it.

My sisters and I often practise basketball in the park.

I also like being at home with my family and having friends over to play. Sometimes we go to Ravenscourt Park and I catch up with my old school friends from Shepherd's Bush.

At home, my sisters help me to read in Dari.

Keeping our culture

At home, we keep up our Afghan culture. We always eat Afghan food for dinner. My favourite meal is *kofta chelo* – meat balls with white rice.

Here are some of our favourite Afghan dishes.

Aushak – pasta stuffed with leeks, in a yogurt sauce

Sabzi – spinach with spices

Kofta – meatballs in lentil and tomato sauce

Mantoo – steamed dumplings in a yogurt sauce

Mixed salad

Qabili pilau – lamb and rice with carrots, raisins and almonds

We celebrate Afghan festivals at home. My family is **Muslim**. My parents and sisters pray at home and we celebrate **Id.**

This year we went to the USA for my uncle's **engagement** party. I wore a Gand Afghani (Afghan dress) with bells around my ankles.

Madina's mum says:

"In Afghanistan in peacetime, there was a funfair at Id and we had a big feast with all the family. Here we hold our celebrations within the family."

Here is my family at the engagement party. The bride-to-be is between my great-grandmother and my grandmother.

My future

We all work hard and aim to do well at school.

Everyone in our family feels settled in Britain and would like to stay here. Ghazal would like to become a doctor. Mina hopes to be a **forensic scientist**. Mum wants to finish her training and find a job in a beauty parlour.

I try my best in everything I do. This week I won an award for doing well in martial arts.

Our Afghan culture is still important. My sisters teach me traditional Afghan dancing.

I want to do really well at school so I can choose my career. If I do go back to Afghanistan in the future, I would like to be Prime Minister! Otherwise, I'd like to be a singer. My plan is also to **foster** a child.

Madina's mum says:

"In Afghanistan, I could only go to school up to year 12. I dreamt of going to university. Now in Britain my daughters are getting a good education."

Glossary

asylum
Protection given to people who have left their country because they were in danger.

beauty therapy
Giving beauty care to people to improve their skin, hair and nails.

burka
A long, loose garment worn by many women in Afghanistan.

civil war
A war between groups of people in the same country.

Dari
The Afghan form of the Iranian language Farsi.

engagement
When two people agree to marry. They sometimes have a party to celebrate.

extended family
A family group that includes parents, children, uncles, aunts and grandparents.

forensic scientist
A person who finds and examines evidence to help solve crimes.

foster
To take somebody else's child into your home to look after him or her.

housing officer
A person who helps to find housing for people in need.

Id
A Muslim festival.

invaded
Entered a country with military force to take it over.

Islamic
Something or someone that belongs to the religion of Islam.

martial arts
One of the fighting sports, including judo and karate.

multicultural
Including people of several different races, religions, languages and traditions.

Muslim
A member of the religion of Islam.

refugees
People who have been forced to leave their own country because it is too dangerous to stay there.

Soviet Union
The former empire, ruled from Moscow in Russia, which stretched from the Baltic and Black Seas to the Pacific Ocean. It lasted from 1922 to 1991.

Taliban
A strict Islamic group that took control of Afghanistan between 1994 and 2001.

Afghanistan fact file

Location: Southern Asia, north and west of Pakistan and east of Iran

Climate: Dry, with cold winters and hot summers

Capital city: Kabul

Population: About 32 million

Life expectancy at birth (the average age people live to): 44

Main religion: Islam

Languages: Mainly Dari and Pashto

Literacy (the percentage of people over 15 who can read and write): 28%

Main jobs: 80% make their living from farming

Number of Afghan refugees: 2.1 million. About one million of these are in neighbouring Pakistan. Around 132,000 Afghans are internally displaced (they have had to leave their homes but are still in Afghanistan)

Index

Further information

BBC News Country Profile – Afghanistan:
http://news.bbc.co.uk/1/hi/world/south_asia/country_profiles/1162668.stm

Growing up in Afghanistan:
http://library.thinkquest.org/CR0212462/

Kids in Afghanistan:
http://teacher.scholastic.com/scholasticnews/indepth/afghanistan_kids

Note to parents and teachers: Please note that these websites are **not** specifically for children and we strongly advise that Internet access is supervised by a responsible adult.